September 22, 1992

To Rita
To help you on the mend.

Love Wendy.

Damiano Bianco-Pepi Merisio

I AM WITH YOU ALWAYS

Originally published as *Ti legherò a me per sempre*
by Edizioni Paoline - Rome (Italy)

The biblical passages were translated
by the Rev. Dr. Ronald Reeve.
The Invitation and the captions beneath the illustrations
were rendered by M. Bryson, L. Morel and B. Morton.

ISBN 0-88840-659-2
Dépôt légal - 3e trimestre 1978
Bibliothèque Nationale du Québec
Bibliothèque Nationale du Canada

EDITIONS PAULINES
250 N. Boul. St-François - Sherbrooke, P. Qué. (Canada)

An Invitation

Seeing... What could be more natural?
Seeing the dawning day
as the sun slowly rises,
and the sheets of colour cover
towns, streets, countryside
and mountain peaks on the horizon.

Seeing is really nothing but
a habit which forms a part
of each day.

Stopping, discovering
rocks, the sea, water, a crow
on the edge of a chimney,

a bending flower,
a tree dancing in the wind.

Seeing, to be moved! To cry,
maybe even laugh with joy
at the beauty of nature's songs.

It is really nothing
only very ordinary; and yet...

And yet, friend, brother, wife, sister,
do you know how to be moved
by water on the falls,
by the fading day,
by the shadow that falls?
I wonder.

I am not even certain of the contrary.

You are so taken, so taken
by time, noise, things to be accomplished:
money to make, holidays to plan,
or work to do.
You are so taken, even enslaved,
that the simplest things
(and the most beautiful),
you know not how to appreciate.

To you I say:
open this book and be moved.

Open the eyes of your heart
and you will rejoice to see
above and beyond yourself.
And you will praise God.

Your heart will overflow
upon Him Who calls to you.
If you listen, come near to Him
and let yourself be moved;
God will meet you,
He will touch your soul.

As a mother takes her child,
so will He take you.
And you, silent, astonished,
will hear the song sung in Paradise.

I leave it with you.
May the Love that surpasses all
fill you with His eternal song.

My Name is Love

I will betroth you to Me for ever,
I will bring you into the wilderness,
I will speak with you tenderly.

Unfaithful as you are!
I will reward you with the good things I have given
And I will make of you the Door of Hope.

You will answer me without selfish designs
As in the days of your youth,
When you escaped to your first exile.

On soaring wings they rise
to meet the light and You, O Lord.

In that day, says the Lord,
My Name shall be Love
And I will no more know any other.

I will betroth you to Me for ever,
In justice and in righteousness,
In loving-kindness and in mercy.

I will betroth you to Myself for ever
And you shall know My Name.

Hosea 2.13-22

An ivy climbs slowly to the uppermost branch of the tree.
Oh, that I might so walk nearer to You, Lord!

Your Word is Worthy of Faith

You are my rock, Lord,
You protect me,
You deliver me, You are my God.
I lean on You,
I take refuge in You,
Mighty Fortress!

When violence tempts me, You deliver me;
My prayers of thanks reach out to You
You have delivered me from my enemies.

In the hollow of the desert of life,
my soul reaches out to You.

You are my lamp, O Lord,
You show me the safe road;
With You I fear nothing,
With you I can dare all things.

O God! Your way is without reproach
And Your Word worthy of praise.
You have given me confidence, O Lord,
To carry Your Name among men.

2 Samuel 22.2-4.29-31

In the depths of the sea, in the depths of solitude,
You are You, eternal God.

I will be a Blessing to you

Go from your country,
Leave your family,
Depart from the house of your parents,
And go to the land that I will show you.

Though the way be straight and narrow,
You guide and direct me: blessed be Your Name forever.

I will bless you,
I will make your name known,
You will be a blessing to all.

I will bless those who bless you,
And those who curse you shall have no peace.
In you shall all the families of the earth
Be blessed.

Genesis 12.1-3

Nothing shall escape Your touch of love,
O Lord! O Father!

It is You who change the hearts

O Lord, God of our fathers!
Make Your Presence known to all this day.
Make me, Your servant,
Not to seek my own advantage,
But only to fulfil Your commands.

Hear me, O Lord,
Give me Your good words
That I may make known
That You are the True God
Who changes hearts.

1 Kings 18.36-37

*Render my heart as clear as these dew drops
in the early morning light.*

I will be Your Guide

I am the Lord, the God of Abraham
And of Isaac, your ancestors.
To you and to your children
I will give a land in which to dwell.

They will be innumerable,
And altogether one
Spread abroad from the North to the South
And from the East to the West.
In you and in your descendant
Shall all the nations of the earth be blessed.

You come to us out of the light and fog
in silence.

Behold! I am with you,
Wherever you go I will keep you.
You shall return to this land;
And until I have done what I have promised,
I will not leave you.

Genesis 28.13-15

As the water reflects the beauty of the sun,
so let my life reflect the beauty of Your goodness.

Solitude

Lord, I fight for You
And my service leaves me without rest.
I see Your children who delight not in Your Love;
Some who deface Your altars,
And others who wish to silence Your prophets.

I alone am left,
And I shall not survive much longer.

*1 Kings 19.*10

*Keep me, O Lord, from a bitter heart,
and leave me in Your love.*

I am your inseparable companion

I am the Inseparable Companion
Of the man who trusts in Me,
Of him whom I have called
In preference to all other.

On him I have breathed my Spirit;
I have made him the bearer of justice.

As the day follows the night from all eternity,
so the Spirit breathes life to the earth.

He does not cry, nor lift up his voice
To be heard in the streets.
He breaks not the bending reed,
He quenches not the flickering flame.
In faithfulness he strives for justice
Without fear of loss
And without compromise,
As long as there is no justice upon earth
And all dissension remains unhealed.

*Isaiah 42.*1-4

*Moss draws its life from the living tree;
let me draw my life from You, Lord.*

Search in the Night

God, who sets the sun to shine in the heavens,
Himself chooses to be found in the darkness.

I have built for You a house!
Be pleased to dwell therein for ever.

1 Kings 8.12-13

*« How beautiful are Your tabernacles,
O Lord of hosts! » (Ps. 84:1).*

God sees through us

Put your trust in God! and persevere at your task;
In the twinkling of an eye,
He can make the poor man rich.

His blessing is enough for the righteous
And he need wait for nothing.

The kiss of leaves in the autumn wind:
a beauty none can surpass.

Do not say: « What do I need?
What else do I desire? ».

Say not: « I have sufficient,
Who can do me harm? ».

In the day of abundance, one forgets evil,
In the day of adversity, one thinks not of good.

Let me stand before You
with as much simplicity as a flower.

It is an easy thing for the Lord
To reward man according to his works
In the last day.
The end of a man reveals the worth of his deeds.
Call no man blessed before his death,
For he is truly known only in his last moments.

Ecclesiasticus 11.21-28

You are here, I am here.
Why do I still thirst?

I love Your living Presence

You, our God, are good and faithful;
Slow to anger, You order all things with kindness.
We are Yours, we know Your power,
And we rest in You, even in our imperfection.
But we would not sin
If we were more attentive,
For to know You is perfect righteousness.
And to know Your mighty Love
Is the beginning of immortality.

The creations of men,
Their shameful idols,
Will never deceive
Those who love Your Living Presence.

Wisdom 15.1-5

Droplets disappear, words are forgotten, forms change;
but You, O Lord, remain from age to age.

It is not easy to follow Me

My son, if you wish to serve the Lord,
You will not have an easy life.
Make for yourself a heart righteous and faithful
Which will not stray in the time of temptation.

At every moment, keep yourself close to God:
He will raise you up in the last day.

Oh, trembling hope that gives life
through all and against all.

Whatever comes, accept it;
In the heights and the depths of your trouble
Be patient.
For gold is tried in the fire, in the crucible,
And the man of God in humiliation.

Put your trust in God;
It is He who shall raise you up.

*Ecclesiasticus 2.*1-6

More pure than the purest gold,
so is the beauty of the Lord.

Everyday someone mocks me

It seems to me, Lord, that You have caught me in a trap
And I have allowed myself to be taken.
You have seized me and You are too strong for me
Every day I am the laughingstock of the people.
Everyone mocks me
Because I must cry out without ceasing:
« Violence and destruction! ».
Every day Your Word becomes for me
Reproach and derision and rejection.

*Life passes, death comes,
but all shall live in You forever.*

If I say myself: « I will reject Him,
I will speak no more in His name».
His word in my heart is a devouring fire
Which burns even into my bones.

I wear myself out trying to ignore Him,
The conflict is intolerable.

*Hold fast to the Lord and take your strength from Him,
even as the ivy takes its vitality from the tree.*

Even my friends watch for my defeat:
«Perhaps he will give way to temptation?
Then we will reduce him to silence
And get him out of the way».
But the Lord is with me, He defends me,
My enemies shall not be able to sing in victory.

Victorious Lord!
You who choose Your partner
And purify him in testing,
Enable me to see my enemies vanquished
And my cause in good hands.

Jeremiah 20.7-12

May I cling to You like the moss to the tree.

I called you from afar

You, my servant, whom I have chosen,
My friend, whom I have brought from afar,
I called you from the ends of the earth;
I said to you: «Be mine.
I have chosen you
I will not abandon you.
Fear not,
For I am your God».

Isaiah 41.8-10

As the shadow flows through the valley,
so let Your kindness be to me, O Father.

You lift up my head

My heart leaps for joy in You, O Lord!
My God, You have made me to hold up my head.
I am able to face my enemies,
I know you will preserve me.
There is none holy as You, O Lord,
Nor any better comforter.

1 Samuel 2.1-3

I am as the buttercup, simple and innocent,
when I am near You, my Lord.

You are prized in my eyes

Fear not, I have redeemed you,
I have given you your name, and you are Mine.
When you pass through deep waters
I will be with you,
They shall not overwhelm you.
When you are passing through fire
The flames will not consume you
Neither shall you burn.
For I, the Lord, I am your God;
You are precious in my sight,
You are worthy of love, and I love you.

Isaiah 43.1-4

In the fires and storms of life,
only You have certain power, O Lord.

How can I thank You

In wretchedness for a very long time
I searched among my brother men
But in vain.
Then I remembered You, Lord,
And Your never-ending affection.
You deliver those who hope in You,
You save them from their enemies.
From the earth I called upon You,
And prayed that I might not falter.

Men have lived here.
You have watched over them
and guided their footsteps.

In my solitude I said: « Lord my Father,
Leave me not in anguish,
To struggle with crushing forces.
I will strive to know Your Name
And joyfully speak Your praises.
You have heard my prayer,
You have saved me from ruin,
You have plucked me from the deep.
I will give You thanks for ever
And carry Your Name in my heart ».

Ecclesiasticus 51.8-12

Men have passed here.
Under Your eye, they knew and loved each other.

Each answers for his love

He who sins shall pay for it;
A son shall not pay for his father
Neither a father for his son.
Each will answer for his love
And each will answer for his conceit.

If the wicked man turns away from his sins,
If he observes all My commandments,
If he acts righteously and justly,
He shall not die, but shall live.
All his sins shall be cancelled out
And his faithfulness shall be his joy
And his reward.

Ezekiel 18.20-22

Songs of life, praise from the earth,
all life sings of Your greatness forever.

Leave me in poverty, Lord

Give me neither poverty nor riches,
But only enough to satisfy my needs.
For if I grow rich I may become
Content without you Lord,
And if I am too poor, I shall become dishonest
And discredit the Name of my God.

Proverbs 30.8-9

I am waiting. Have You forgotten me?
Oh, how I long for Your return!

Do not ignore your brothers

Stop being accomplices of evil,
Free yourselves from bondage to impurity,
From your customary habits.
Promote the freedom of others
And put an end to all trickery.

Share your bread with the hungry,
Open your doors to the friendless,
Give clothing to those who need it,
And delight not in separating yourself
From your brothers.

Songs of the world, songs of the waves,
songs of the men who praise You.
You answer those who listen.

Then shall shine forth radiantly
The light of your human spirit.
You shall be healed of your greediness,
And justice shall go before you
With the glory of the Lord.

You will call and He will answer you,
You will cry out and He will say: « Here I am! ».
If you will put away all unworthy bondage
And cease to speak and to judge in vain.

Isaiah 58.6-9

The water ripples quietly through the bulrushes.
You remember the lives of those who love You.

You are always right, Lord

You are always right, Lord,
And I cannot dispute with You.
I ask only this of You:
How is it that the wicked prosper?
Why do the treacherous live in peace?
You have planted them like trees,
They take root, they flourish, they bear fruit.
Always they have Your Name in their mouths
But it is not in their hearts.
But You, Lord, You know me, You see me,
And You know well that my heart is with You.

Jeremiah 12.1-3

As the great tree speaks of Your glory,
so my soul praises You.

I am your point of reference

Do not lose courage, neither tremble.
You have seen how the Lord your God has cared for you
As a father cares for his child.

Yet you have not trusted the Lord your God
Who goes before you in the way
To prepare the stages of your journey.

In the night, He is like a fiery beacon
Who shows you the right path,
And by day, like a cloud, He shades you.

Deuteronomy 1.31-33

Of what use are the walls and barriers of man?
You are there.

Your Name is Hope

Lord, Your Name is Hope;
Those who forsake You lose their bearings,
Those who flee from meeting You
Are but as foot-prints in the sand,
And barren dryness travels with them.

*Jeremiah 17.*13

Caught in the whirlwind of this mad joyous dance,
we are always protected by our Father's love.

I probe the hearts

Blessed is the man who puts his trust in God,
And has made the Lord his hope.
He is like a tree on the riverbank,
Whose roots drink deeply from the stream
Never suffering from the great heat.
His leaves shall be always green,
And never withering
He shall give his fruit for ever.

As the weeping willow sheds its tear upon the water,
so my soul longs for You.

The heart is deceitful, above all things,
Impossible of healing;
Who, then, can know it?
— I, the Lord, I probe the hearts,
I test their motives,
I give to each according to his works,
According to the fruit of his actions.

Jeremiah 17.7-10

As the lily pad floats on shadow,
so my heart waits for You.

Your Name is Friend

If our sins witness against us, Lord,
Act for the honour of Your Name.
Our rebellions have been many
And our sins against You innumerable.

O our hope,
You Who save from distress,
Why are you absent from us
Like a wayfarer who passes on?

As the infinite wind whispers in the plain,
so You speak in our hearts in language unknown.

Why are you withdrawn, Lord,
As though incapable of saving?
Remain with us,
Go not away!
Let Your Name be for us « Friend »;
Leave us not alone!

Jeremiah 14.7-9

O Light, O Brilliance, O Silence,
penetrate my heart forever.

My Ways are not your ways

Search for the Lord, for He wants to be found,
Call upon Him, for He is near.
When the wicked man changes direction,
And the unrighteous man changes his mind,
They will be converted to the Lord,
And He will receive them with love.

O most Powerful One, teach me to be humble
in Your presence.

My thoughts are not your thoughts,
Says the Lord,
And My ways are not your ways.
As far as the heavens are from the earth
So far are My ways from your ways
And My thoughts from your thoughts.

Isaiah 55.6-9

In the depths, the very depths of life,
You may be hidden, but You are always there.

Bring me back to You

You have corrected me with suffering
And I understood that this was just,
As a calf accepts its yoke.
Turn me back again
To the pathway
That leads to you, my Lord.

I have taken the wrong road,
I know it, and I have made amends.
I am ashamed and confused
At the foolishness of my youth.

Jeremiah 31.18-19

*The song of rock and light
cries out to the glory of God.*

I am an exacting God

Chase from your heart the taste for oppression,
The menacing gesture, the hurtful word.
Share your bread with the hungry,
Restore the oppressed.
Then, your light will shine in the darkness
And even the shadows will glisten as the day.

Hidden, yet never failing:
this is the way of Your Spirit, Lord.

The Lord will be your Guide for ever,
He will nourish you in the arid desert,
He will give you strength.

You will be like a well-watered garden,
A never-failing well of water.

May Your love, like the rushing water,
fall on me, Lord.

You will rebuild the ancient ruins,
You will establish the future generations,
You shall be known as the one who repairs the breaches
And restores broken houses.

Isaiah 58.9-12

As the water murmurs in the crystal sounds,
so You speak to me in words unheard of.

Let your heaven be in my eyes

Lord, Father and Master of my life,
Abandon me not to the caprice of hollow words,
Nor let me be lost in them.
Who will keep guard over my thoughts,
And help me to speak nothing haphazardly?
That the beguiling of my intellect
Cause not my loss;
That my errors might not increase.
Neither my faults multiply themselves.
Leave me not to fall into the hands
Of those who play with words,
Neither give them this pleasure.

Life eternal begins and death shall never reign.

Lord, Father and God of my life,
Preserve my gaze pure and alert
That Your heaven may be in my eyes.
Lest sensuality or lust overtake me,
Leave me not under the control of shameless desire.

Ecclesiasticus 23.1-6

Consider a mountain lake. Not the things it reflects.
Consider its transparency.

I have shown you My Face

God made man of the earth,
And will return him to it at the end.

He gives him the number of his days,
A fixed time for the domination of the earth.
He gives him power to defend himself
And a face like to His own.

All living things fear man,
The master of the savage beasts and the birds.

Even a fallen leaf speaks of Your glory, Lord.

The Lord has made with men
An eternal covenant.
He has shown them a sure road.
He has said to them: «Keep yourselves
From injustice».
He has set them their task:
That each should think of his neighbour.

Ecclesiasticus 17.1-14

The fusion of gold and silence in the embrace of autumn.
This is Your wisdom.

Your works are marvellous

Lord, You are my God,
I honor and praise Your Name,
For You have done wonderful things,
True to your marvellous word.

When You pass by, the desert begins to bloom.

Lord! be the defender of the poor,
A refuge for the needy in his distress;
A strong shelter from the storm,
A cool shade from the heat.

Though the mighty blasts of the hurricane
Scorch the dry earth in the sun,
Bring their insolences to an end
As a cloud masks the sun;
Take from them their taste for oppression.

Isaiah 25.1-5

The rocks sing like living water,
because You are my refuge forever.

You will hunger for My Word

Listen, you who crush the poor
And drive out the disinherited!
You who say: «When is the best time
To sell our grain at the highest price?
And when will it be a seller's market,
That we may use false weights and measures
To purchase the dignity of the poor?».
In that day, says the Lord,
I will clean you out with the tempest,
I will turn your feasts into mourning
And your songs will sing of sadness.

Let my heart be silent to listen to You, Lord.

Behold, the days come, says the Lord,
When greed shall give birth to famine, —
Not hunger for bread, nor thirst for water, —
But hunger and thirst for the Word of God;
And none shall speak it any more.

Amos 8.4-12

The hunger of the sea is limited by the shore,
but my hunger for You, Lord, knows no bounds.

Be my hope always

Heal me, Lord, and I shall be healed,
Save me, that I may be saved,
You are my hope.

They mock me, they say to me:
«Where is the Word of God?
What is it accomplishing?».
Yet I have not pressed for the worst,
I have not desired misery, You know it.
You know well what words I have said.
Let this not be the cause of my downfall,
You Whom I have chosen for my refuge in evil days.

Those who scoff at me,
They are shameful, not me!
They are fearful, not me!
Let them be punished, as is just.

*Jeremiah 17.*14-18

My rock, my shelter, my fortress!
In You I build my love.

No more am I unknown

The rain and the snow come down from heaven
And return not without having watered the earth,
Making it fruitful and fertile.
Even so, the word coming out of My mouth
Does not return to Me fruitlessly,
Without having done that which I wish,
And accomplishes My purpose.

Isaiah 55.10-11

You are here.
You are listening to me.
You are watching over me.

I do what I can, Lord

Lord, to Whom nothing can remain unknown,
Remember me, concern Yourself with me,
Defend me against those who wish me ill.
Abandon me not,
I suffer great anguish for You.
When I came to know Your Word,
I devoured it.
How marvellous it was to hear You!
Even yet I have the joy of being called
By Your Name.

How wonderful it is to be there in silence!

Lord, my trusted Guide,
Never have I taken part in useless assemblies,
In sterile disputes.
Knowing Your strength,
I continued to speak with You alone,
Having no taste for mere verbiage.
Why must I suffer without ceasing?
Why languish like an incurable?
Will You be to me a mirage,
Deceitful water that quenches not my thirst?

Jeremiah 15.15-18

Shadow and light, hope of the night:
all things come to an end and life begins again.

It is I who give you tongue

A voice says to me: « Cry! ».
And I answer: « What must I cry? ».
Every creature is but as grass
And all its beauty is as the flower of the field.
The grass withers, the flower droops
When the Spirit of God blows upon it.
The grass withers, the flower fades,
But the Word of God lasts forever.

Isaiah 40.6-8

*The grass will become verdant in the eternal Spring,
and the trees will bear fruit forever.*

Dialogue

O Lord, Who only is adorable!
Here I am!
I will not let You go
Until You have blessed me!
I pray You, tell me Your Name.

Baruch 6.6; Isaiah 58.9; Genesis 32.27-30

An open window, a glance, a light, a Presence.
You are always there.